What's in this book

This book belongs to

_____

我比你高 I am taller than you

学习内容 Contents

生词 New words

★	高	tall
★	矮	short
★	个子	height
★	脸	face
★	圆	round
★	方	square
★	比	than
	哥哥	elder brother
	肚子	belly
	好看	good-looking

句式 Sentence patterns

我比你高。你比我矮。

I am taller than you. You are shorter than me.

文化 Cultures

历史上伟大的人物
Great people in history

跨学科学习 Project

了解并计算体重指数
Learn about the body mass
index (BMI) and calculate it

Get ready

1 How tall are you?

2 Who is the tallest student in your class?

3 Who is taller, Ethan or Ivan?

比 bǐ

哥哥 gē ge

高 gāo

矮 ǎi

"哥哥，我比你高，你比我矮。"艾文说。

"你们的个子一样高。"
浩浩说。

liǎn
脸

fāng
方

yuán
圆

"伊森的脸方，艾文的
脸圆。"浩浩又说。

"浩浩，你看我们比你高多少呢?"艾文问。

hǎo kàn
好看

"你们比我高，但我比
你们好看！"浩浩说。

dù zi
肚子

"是啊，浩浩的脸圆，
肚子也圆。"艾文说。

Let's think

1 Recall the story. Put a tick or a cross.

2 How tall are you? Draw below.

你多高?

New words

1 Learn the new words.

比　个子　好看　高　脸　哥哥　矮　肚子　方　圆

2 Look and complete the sentences. Write the letters.

a 比　b 圆　c 高　d 矮　e 脸　f 个子

1 他＿＿＿高，＿＿＿方。

2 她脸＿＿＿，个子不＿＿＿。

3 她＿＿＿他＿＿＿。

听听说说 Listen and say

🎧 03 **1** Listen and circle the correct pictures.

🎧 04 **2** Look at the pictures. Listen to the st

1

2

3

①

矮个子在前面，高个子在后面。

③

你们圆圆的脸，比红苹果好看。

d say.

我比你高，我在后面。

3 Talk about the stationery family with your friend. Use these words.

比　高　矮　圆

方　脸　个子

尺子爸爸……

笔妈妈……

本子哥哥……

橡皮妹妹……

Task

Find out who the two tallest boys and girls are in your class.
Draw and say.

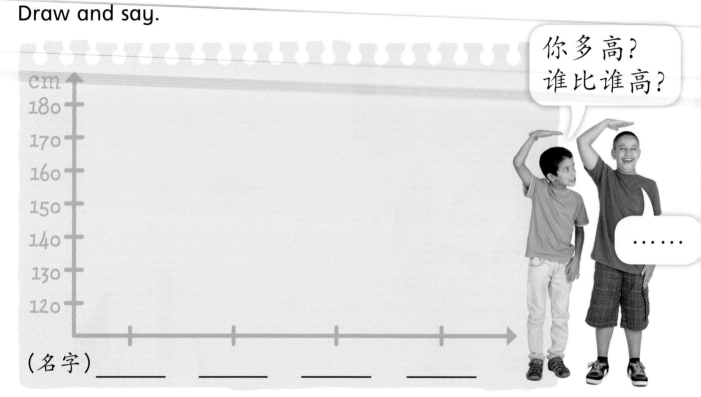

cm
180
170
160
150
140
130
120

（名字）＿＿＿＿　＿＿＿＿　＿＿＿＿　＿＿＿＿

你多高？
谁比谁高？

......

Game

Listen to your teacher and help Hao Hao complete the sentences.

这个苹果
......

这个苹果	那个苹果	大
蛋糕	糖果	好吃
果汁	茶	好喝
红本子	蓝本子	好看
姐姐	我	高
弟弟	哥哥	矮
男孩	女孩	多
橡皮	铅笔	少

这个苹果比
那个苹果大。

Song

Listen and sing.

你的个子高不高？
她的脸儿圆不圆？
我们比一比。

你的个子高，
她的脸儿圆，
我的肚子大，

大家不一样，
大家都好看。

课堂用语 Classroom language

我忘记了。
I forgot.

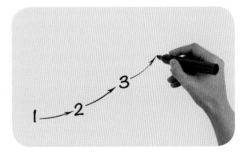

接下来，……
Next, …

写一写 Write

1 Learn and trace the stroke.

竖提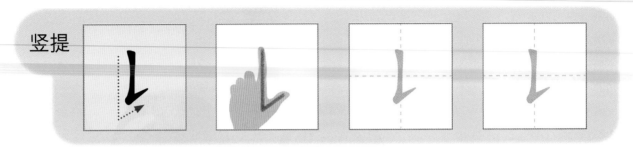

2 Learn the components. Colour 比 red and 高 green in the characters.

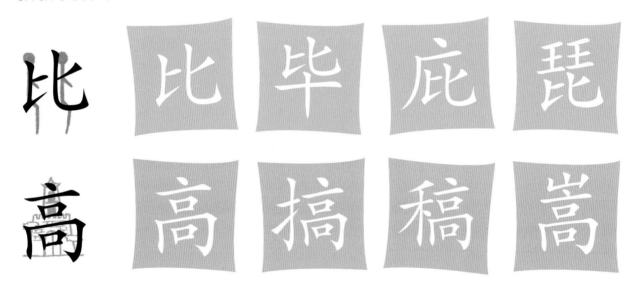

比

比 毕 庇 琵

高

高 搞 稿 嵩

3 Look at the words carefully. Tick the correct sentences.

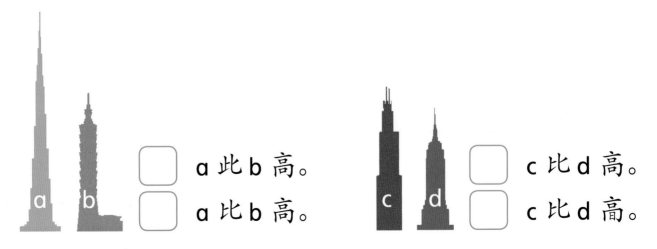

☐ a 此 b 高。

☐ a 比 b 高。

☐ c 比 d 高。

☐ c 比 d 髙。

4 Trace and write the characters.

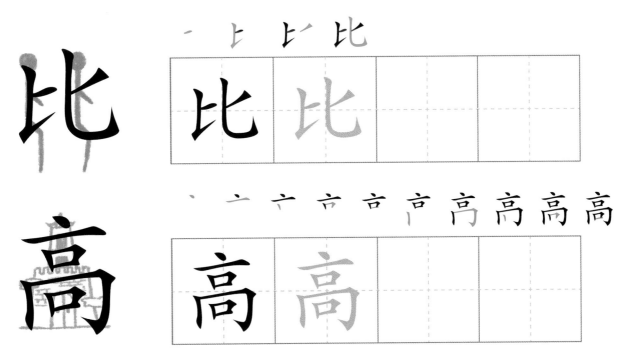

5 Write and say.

我 ☐ 哥哥矮。

我 ☐ 妹妹 ☐ 。

汉字小常识 *Did you know?*

Colour the component that encloses another component red.

Some characters include a component which encloses another component on three sides — left, right and bottom.

   医 匚

Cultures

1 Statues are built to honour great people in history. Match the names to the photos. Write the letters.

a Abraham Lincoln

b Aristotle

c Genghis Khan

d Napoleon

e Queen Victoria

2 Find out about a great man or woman in your country. Complete the table and tell your friend about him/her.

Paste a photo here

国家：	名字：

他／她叫 _____。

他／她的个子 _____。

他／她的脸 _____。

1 Have you heard of the body mass index (BMI)? Find out how it works and talk about it.

BMI shows us whether we are overweight or underweight in relation to our height.

$$BMI = \frac{weight\ (kg)}{height\ (metre)\ \times\ height\ (metre)}$$

你的 BMI 是多少？

15.2

21.0

 Your BMI

我的 BMI 是……，比你的 BMI 高吗？

18.8

Your weight: _____ kg
Your height: _____ m
Result (kg/m²): _____

17.9

2 Different countries sometimes have different BMI standards. Find out the standards in your country and compare your BMI with them.

我的 BMI

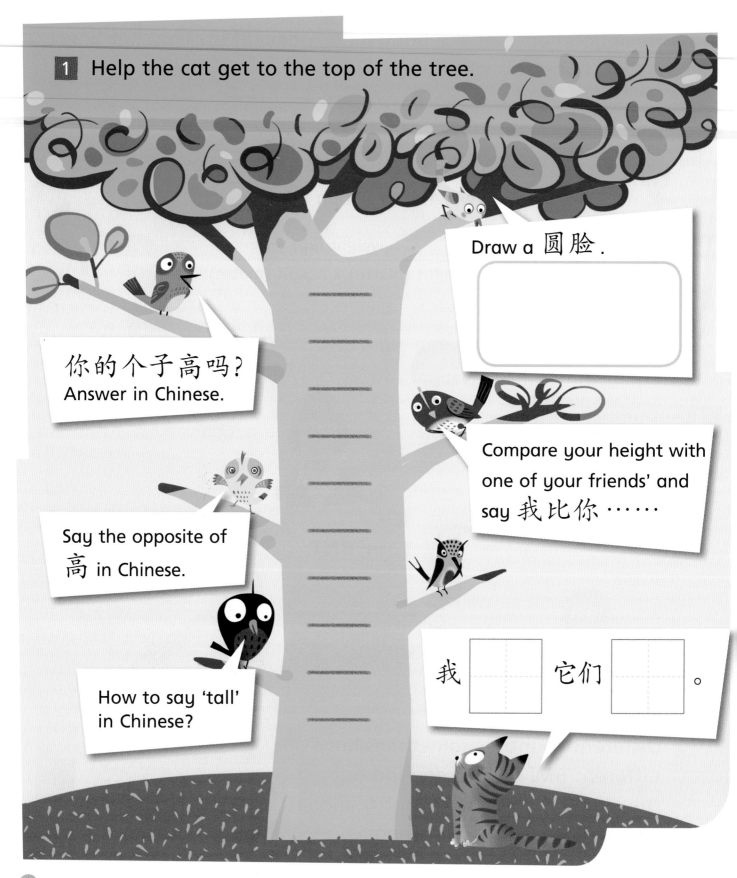

Help the cat get to the top of the tree.

Draw a 圆脸.

你的个子高吗?
Answer in Chinese.

Say the opposite of 高 in Chinese.

How to say 'tall' in Chinese?

Compare your height with one of your friends' and say 我比你……

我 ⬜⬜ 它们 ⬜⬜ 。

0

2 Work with your friend. Colour the stars and the chillies.

Words	说	读	写
高	☆	☆	☆
矮	☆	☆	🌶
个子	☆	☆	🌶
脸	☆	☆	🌶
圆	☆	☆	🌶
方	☆	☆	🌶
比	☆	☆	☆
哥哥	☆	🌶	🌶
肚子	☆	🌶	🌶
好看	☆	🌶	🌶

Sentences	说	读	写
他的脸圆，肚子也圆。	☆	🌶	🌶
我比你高，你比我矮。	☆	☆	🌶

Describe someone's physical appearance	☆
Compare heights	☆

3 What does your teacher say?

My teacher says …

Words I remember

高	gāo	tall
矮	ǎi	short
个子	gè zi	height
脸	liǎn	face
圆	yuán	round
方	fāng	square
比	bǐ	than
哥哥	gē ge	elder brother
肚子	dù zi	belly
好看	hǎo kàn	good-looking

Other words

一样	yī yàng	same
又	yòu	again
但	dàn	but
啊	a	(used at the end of a sentence to express agreement)

OXFORD
UNIVERSITY PRESS

Oxford University Press is a department of the University of Oxford.
It furthers the University's objective of excellence in research, scholarship,
and education by publishing worldwide. Oxford is a registered trade mark of
Oxford University Press in the UK and in certain other countries

Published in Hong Kong by
Oxford University Press (China) Limited
39th Floor, One Kowloon, 1 Wang Yuen Street, Kowloon Bay,
Hong Kong

Illustrated by Anne Lee, KK Ng, KY Chan and Wildman

Photographs for reproduction permitted by Dreamstime.com

China National Publications Import & Export (Group) Corporation is an authorized distributor of
Oxford Elementary Chinese.

Please contact content@cnpiec.com.cn or 86-10-65856782

ISBN: 978-0-19-082198-2

10 9 8 7 6 5 4 3 2